EASY JAZZ FAVORITES

15 Selections For Young Jazz Ensembles

Contents

Title	Arranger	Page
Ain't Misbehavin'	Lowden	2
All The Things You Are	Sweeney	4
Blue Train (Blue Trane)	Sweeney	6
Caravan	Sweeney	8
Chameleon	Sweeney	10
Fly Me To The Moon (In Other Words)	Nowak	12
The Girl From Ipanema	Berry	14
In The Mood	Sweeney	16
Inside Out	Sweeney	18
Milestones	Blair	20
A Nightingale Sang In Berkeley Square	Holmes	22
One Note Samba	Nowak	24
Route 66	Sweeney	26
St. Louis Blues	Sweeney	28
When I Fall In Love	Holmes	30

HAL•LEONARD®
CORPORATION

7777 W. BLUEMOUND RD. P.O. BOX 13819 MILWAUKEE, WI 53213

AIN'T MISBEHAVIN'

Words by ANDY RAZAF
Music by THOMAS WALLER and HARRY BROOKS
Arranged by BOB LOWDEN

ALTO SAX 2

ALTO SAX 2

ALL THE THINGS YOU ARE
(From VERY WARM FOR MAY)

Lyrics by OSCAR HAMMERSTEIN II
Music by JEROME KERN
Arranged by MICHAEL SWEENEY

ALTO SAX 2

ALTO SAX 2

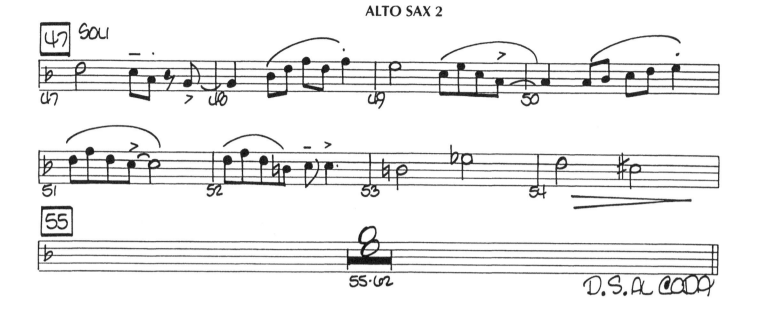

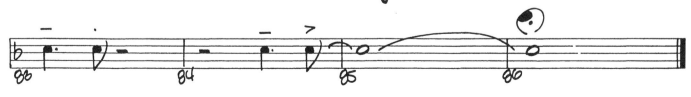

BLUE TRAIN
(Blue Trane)

ALTO SAX 2

By JOHN COLTRANE
Arranged by MICHAEL SWEENEY

ALTO SAX 2

CARAVAN
(From SOPHISTICATED LADIES)

Words and Music by DUKE ELLINGTON,
IRVING MILLS and JUAN TIZOL
Arranged by MICHAEL SWEENEY

Alto Sax 2

CHAMELEON

ALTO SAX 2

By HERBIE HANCOCK, PAUL JACKSON,
HARVEY MASON and BENNIE MAUPIN
Arranged by MICHAEL SWEENEY

ALTO SAX 2

FLY ME TO THE MOON
(In Other Words)

ALTO SAX 2

Words and Music by BART HOWARD
Arranged by JERRY NOWAK

ALTO SAX 2

THE GIRL FROM IPANEMA
(Garôta De Ipanema)

ALTO SAX 2

Original Words by VINICIUS DE MORAES
Music by ANTONIO CARLOS JOBIM
Arranged by JOHN BERRY

IN THE MOOD

Alto Sax 2

By JOE GARLAND
Arranged by MICHAEL SWEENEY

INSIDE OUT

ALTO SAX 2

By MICHAEL SWEENEY

ALTO SAX 2

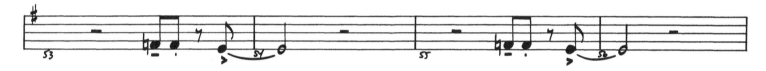

MILESTONES

ALTO SAX 2

By MILES DAVIS
Arranged by PETER BLAIR

ALTO SAX 2

D.S. AL CODA
(W/REPEAT)

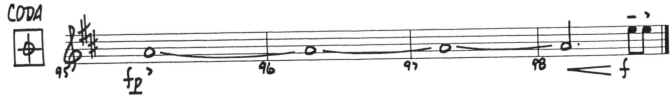

A NIGHTINGALE SANG
IN BERKELEY SQUARE

Lyric by ERIC MASCHWITZ
Music by MANNING SHERWIN
Arranged by ROGER HOLMES

Alto Sax 2

ALTO SAX 2

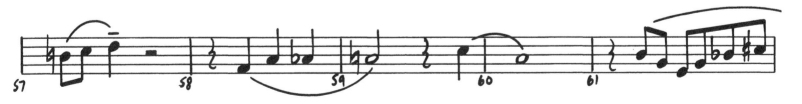

ONE NOTE SAMBA
(Samba De Uma Nota So)

ALTO SAX 2

Original Lyrics by NEWTON MENDONCA
English Lyrics by ANTONIO CARLOS JOBIM
Music by ANTONIO CARLOS JOBIM
Arranged by JERRY NOWAK

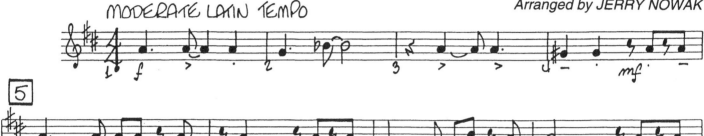

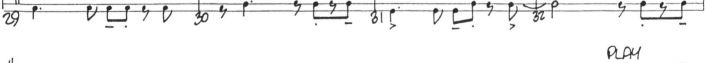

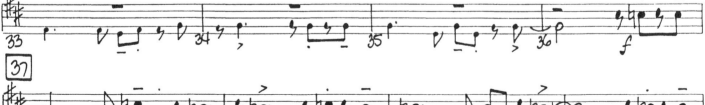

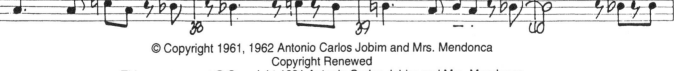

MCA music publishing

ROUTE 66

Alto Sax 2

By BOBBY TROUP
Arranged by MICHAEL SWEENEY

ALTO SAX 2

ST. LOUIS BLUES

ALTO SAX 2

Words and Music by W.C. HANDY
Arranged by MICHAEL SWEENEY

ALTO SAX 2

WHEN I FALL IN LOVE

Words by EDWARD HEYMAN
Music by VICTOR YOUNG
Arranged by ROGER HOLMES

Alto Sax 2

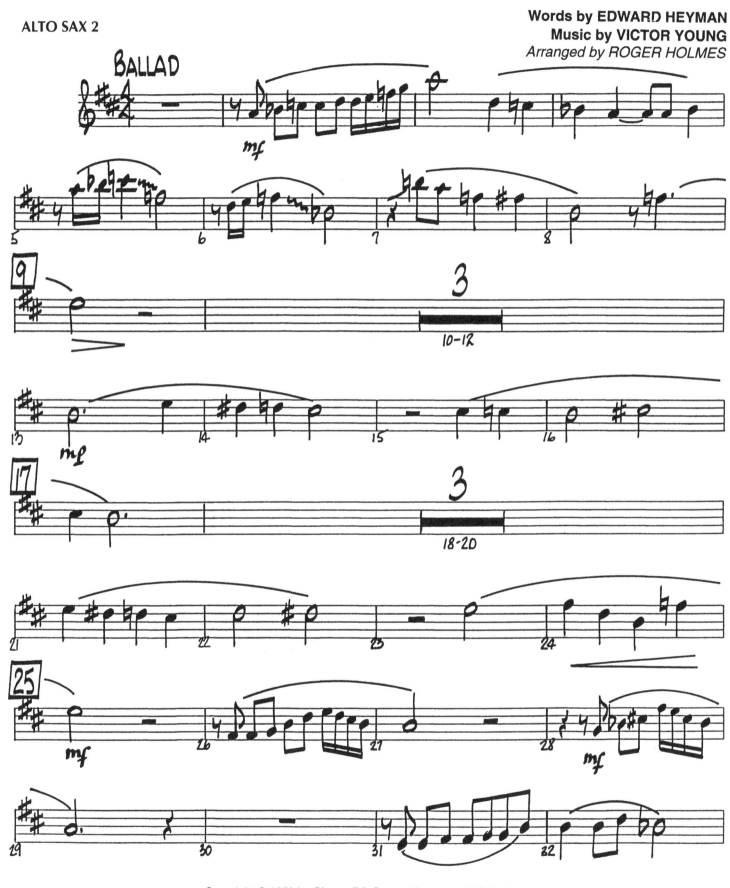

ALTO SAX 2